The Quiet Eye

THIRTEEN WAYS
OF LOOKING AT NATURE

Edited by
Mary Junge, Joyce Kennedy,
Ilze Kļaviņa Mueller, and Tom Ruud

LAUREL
POETRY
COLLECTIVE

ACKNOWLEDGMENTS: "Small Lament, Midsummer" and "The Waiting," by Lisa Ann Berg, previously published in *Coming Back to the World* (Laurel Poetry Collective, 2005); "Beautiful," "The Sun Sits Down," and "Paired," by Annie Breitenbucher, in *Fortune* (Laurel Poetry Collective, 2006); "Beloved Is like a Perfect Day," "Buddha, Egret," and "Death Is the Innermost Hunter," by Su Smallen, in *Weight of Light* (Laurel Poetry Collective, 2004), "Snow That Falls like Amnesia" in *Packingtown Review*, "November 3, 2004 / What Prevails" and "Kinds of Snow" in *Water~Stone Review*; "One Day," by Nolan Zavoral, in *The Heretic Hotel* (Laurel Poetry Collective, 2007).

© 2009 by Laurel Poetry Collective

All rights reserved.

ISBN 978-0-9787973-4-8

Printed in the United States of America.

Published by Laurel Poetry Collective

1168 Laurel Avenue, St. Paul MN 55104

www.laurelpoetry.com

Cover photo © Linda Gammell: "Prairie Rose," from the "Field Guide: Prairies" portfolio

Photos on page 74 © Annie Breitenbucher

Book design by Sylvia Ruud

Library of Congress Cataloging-in-Publication Data

The quiet eye : thirteen ways of looking at nature / edited by Mary Junge, Joyce Kennedy, Ilze Klavina Mueller, and Tom Ruud.
 p. cm.
 ISBN 978-0-9787973-4-8 (alk. paper)
 1. Nature—Poetry. 2. American poetry—21st century. I. Junge, Mary.
PS595.N22Q54 2009
811'.608036—dc22
　　　　　　　　　　　　　　　　　　　　　　　　2009048381

THE QUIET EYE

Other publications by the Laurel Poetry Collective:

A New Name for the Sun (anthology)
Once a World, Yvette Nelson
Gate, Ilze Kļaviņa Mueller
Come Now to the Window, Ann Iverson
Miscellaneous, Tender, Susanna Styve
Burning, Teresa Boyer
Diamonds on the Back of a Snake, Pam Wynn
Pulling for Good News (anthology)
Pilgrim Eye, Mary L. Junge
Between the Houses, Margot Fortunato Galt
In the Tent Called Amazement, Nancy Walden
Weight of Light, Su Smallen
Coming Back to the World, Lisa Ann Berg
Bluefire (anthology)
House of Music, Suzanne Swanson
Where the Moon Is, Lois Welshons
Unable for the World to Sleep, Tom Ruud
Ghost Lamp, Joyce Kennedy
Ignited (anthology)
Soundings, Georgia A. Greeley
Excerpts from Girl, Eileen O'Toole
Kingdoms, Deborah Keenan
Fortune, Annie Breitenbucher
The Heretic Hotel, Nolan Zavoral

CONTENTS

Introduction   xi
    Tom Ruud

Ilze Klaviņa Mueller

Eye	5
Easy to Please a Dog	6
Sunday at the Dam	7
Animal Kingdom	8
Did He Love	9
Our Race's Finest Failure	10

Tom Ruud

Voyageurs	13
Confirmation Class	14
Anima Mundi: Four Possible Paintings	15
A Nature Poem	16
Bad Boy	17
Two Current Versions	18

Lisa Ann Berg

Small Lament, Midsummer	21
Small Idyll	22
Here Now	24
This Day	25
Small Redemption	26
The Waiting	27

Suzanne Swanson

plain	31
1981, 2008	32
Beach 4	33
Best Guess	34
Death Tries to Teach Her	35
Some Days	36

Mary Junge

The Water Carried	39
Girl Putting Away the Lily Pond for Winter	40
Mount Rainer, 2008	41
Last Night	42
Dedication, Darwin Day, 2009	43
The Passage	45

Margot Fortunato Galt

She Wanted	49
She Meant	50
Prairie Rose Hips: Autumn	51
Common Mullein	52
summer drives	53
Lake Drought	54

Su Smallen

Beloved Is like a Perfect Day	59
Death Is the Innermost Hunter	60
Buddha, Egret	64
Snow That Falls like Amnesia	65
November 3, 2004 / What Prevails	66
Kinds of Snow	67

Annie Breitenbucher

My Father at Sunset	73
This Is My Story	74
Last ride	75
Beautiful	76
Paired	77
The Sun Sits Down	78

Nancy Walden

Boundary Waters	81
White	82
Hummingbird	83
Map and Drum	84
Humpback Whale	85
Sandhill Crane	86

Ann Iverson

Reckless	89
All These Butterflies	90
The Great Blue Heron	92
Day Lily and the Sparrow	93
Her Job at Dusk While a Storm Threatens	94
To Know a Snow Angel	95

Nolan Zavoral

Introductions	99
Funky Little Poem	100
Petition	101
Jane's Garden	102
One Day	103
66	104

Eileen O'Toole

    Summer, Earth   107

    In the Wake of the Flood We Pitch Our Tents   108

    Cinque Terre   109

    Monkeys of Tambopata   110

Joyce Kennedy

    Our Daughter Writes from Across the World   113

    Nine Great Egrets   114

    It Quickens the Heart   115

    Cricket   116

    How We, Too, Became Hermits   117

    Mid-October   119

Introduction

LAUREL POETRY COLLECTIVE welcomes you to this new collection of poems by its members. We thirteen have accepted the invitation, the challenge, to address ourselves as poets and citizens of the world to a very broad topic: Nature. The results are collected here. As an added challenge, the invitation asked the poets to provide a brief or an extensive preface to their group of poems, a prose remark intended to cast additional light from a different angle onto their work, thoughts, feelings, fears, and inspirations with regard to nature.

Nature loves to hide. —Heraclitus, 6th Century BCE

If Heraclitus is right—and surely he is—then we Laurels have sent out our own small search party, one that has scouted out a surprising variety of pathways to nature's keep. Seventy-six poems make treks into where we are, have been, or may go. With a quiet eye, observations were brought into clarity, turned this way and that, and brought home to this book. And it turns out that no single theme or approach has prevailed. There is every kind of nature poem here, from lyric to narrative, from the objective to the highly personal, from poems of wonderment to those of warning, from poems set in wilderness and prairie to cityscapes and dreamscapes. The environment and its perils sit shoulder to shoulder with the beautiful and the spiritual. Hope, most of all, stood behind all our efforts. Thus, for the reader, we wish this book to be received as a multifaceted talisman of enduring hope in these times.

—Tom Ruud, Coeditor

*For Deborah Keenan—poet, teacher, and friend—
whose voice and vision made the Laurel Poetry Collective a reality.*

Besides the poets and graphic artists whose work appears in this book, other founding members of the Laurel Poetry Collective were Teresa Boyer, Georgia A. Greeley, Deborah Keenan, Yvette Nelson, Regula Russelle, Susanna Styve, Lois Welshons, and Pam Wynn.

Ilze Kļaviņa Mueller

As my poems attest, I come from a Northeastern European tradition where men and women and children spend days every summer and fall roaming the woods and fields in search of herbs, berries, and mushrooms. I learned the names of plants and fungi and their uses at my mother's knee and, naming them, learned to love them deeply. Sadly, and with a lot of anger, I have watched familiar wild places near my various homes in Minnesota vanish, give way to warehouses surrounded by lawn, condos and their sterile landscaping, strip malls and parking lots. I've watched birds and insects and animals vanish as their habitats shrink and disappear. My work celebrates what is left of the wild in our all too urban world: the unstructured, unexpected, stubborn life that exists in spite of the standardized and boringly predictable outgrowths of what goes by the name of civilization.

My work is modeled to some extent on the folk songs of my Latvian ancestors. The songs are in my bones, and unfortunately they are untranslatable (a great frustration for me). They are rooted in the natural cycles we city dwellers have almost forgotten. The closest I can get to the rural lives of my foremothers and forefathers is to strive for simplicity, sober honesty, and directness in my poems, to remind my readers that there is a world still accessible to us which nourishes our souls, to warn them that, once lost, trees and birds of prey and beetles and water creatures are irreplaceable, and that this loss will be the doom of the human race. I still hope that it's not too late, that somehow we will be able to save the precious ecosystems of our Earth. As a poet, I am glad I can be one of the voices that speak for the fragile, miraculous manifestations of life everywhere on this planet.

EYE
After seeing Allan Bray's Cheese Factory Spring

There is a forest where trees
have mouths and speak
to woodsmen when they come
with axes. There winter is only
a state of mind, and the earth
opens its eye, blinks
its green lashes, declares spring
has arrived. The branches
mirrored in that pool of eye
are swept by warm winds
and if we dive in, you and I,
our skin will lose its wrinkles,
our joints their aches.
We'll laugh and play like otters.
No one will think to look for us,
for the snow shows
no trace of footsteps. The quiet
eye that only opens every
thousand years has closed
its lid. Blue drifts lie
under bare trees, and they won't tell.

EASY TO PLEASE A DOG

Quiet ecstasy. It rained for hours and all that rain has woken months' worth of smells that the dog must now discover and rediscover: Bored is not in her vocabulary. With serious delight, inch by inch, she studies the length of the city block. Like kids who will always remember the ice cream on the square outside the ancient cathedral they saw during the vacation but are unimpressed by the building itself, she focuses on the little things: a clump of grass, the flick of a squirrel's tail, an invisible trail of scent on a patch of asphalt. They say Casals played the same Bach prelude and fugue every morning for over eighty years. No glazed eyes for him: something new with each repetition. How is an old dog like an aged world-famous cellist? What is this, hidden deep inside, like a glinting coal under layers of gray ashes? What would the world be like if we let it go cold?

SUNDAY AT THE DAM

This page would have to be pretty long
to show us crossing the river.
The paper would have to be tough
to withstand the wind, the drizzle of rain,
the suck of the water rolling, rolling
brown as cedar swamps up north.
Would there be room to put in the green
buds of the plums on the bank, the boys
fishing below the dam? On the powerlines
the pigeons sit by threes and fours.
A couple of mallards go flapping
across the gray sky.
                            You point out the place
where Mishka, grinning eagerly as only
dogs grin, had her picture taken
when she was young and strong—she's
one hundred and five in human years now,
but still bounds up to lick our salty hands.

They say animals feel no self-pity.
On this Sunday, I long to bound like an old
dog, learn balance from pigeons, endurance
from ducks. If the wind blows me over the dam,
with my black umbrella, like that hard to believe
British nanny, I want to float in the clouds.

ANIMAL KINGDOM

In your backyard, the goshawk rules now
Sits on the pile of brushwood
Surveys the snowy scene:
Two half-eaten ducks, a drake
Bereft, confused, looking for his dead wives.
The goshawk's head is big and round.
Sternly he stares and stares.
His eyes are fixed on you.
Nothing malignant. A steady presence.
Yesterday you waved your arms
Shouted. You know he wants that drake.
You almost left a chicken you had bought
As sacrifice or bribe. Then changed your mind.
You watch him from your window, your cheek
Against your fosterbaby's soft black hair.
You will him to be gone, you want it back—
The pond, two hen mallards waddling by their mate,
Squirrels chasing each other up an elm,
The loud and normal conversation of the crows.

After seeing a painting by Marsden Hartley

DID HE LOVE

this valley, held by mountains that kept out
the light in early mornings? Did he go out
at noon to paint when the land lay
open to the sun and the trees were less somber
on the shore? Perhaps this restricted
palette challenged him: everything muted. The firs
almost black, the distant alders livid, bruised,
except where he allowed himself
a touch of yellow at the water's edge. The lake
pale as old ice, barely ruffled by a breeze.
And then he looked up, saw chilly blue
but stubbornly added the clouds:
barely visible the gold that made the landscape smile
so that all, all seemed hopeful and it was clear
the birds (mere tick marks high above the cove)
were coming back for one more spring.

OUR RACE'S FINEST FAILURE

Always touting progress
as though regress had no virtue

as though circle dances
were a waste of time

as though back and forth
up and down were boring

Today, friend, join me
let's walk through the woods

Rest assured we'll return
to our starting point

Maybe we'll find some berries
a mushroom by the path

One thing is certain
We're bound to get tired

Your heart will hammer
my knees will hurt like hell

We'll sit on benches
built by kind volunteers

Our eyes will slurp green
our ears the rush of the wind

I'll ask you the name of the bird
that swoops and rises
swoops and rises over the trees

The bird makes no progress
Who knows what it thinks
I'd say it's drunk with bliss

Tom Ruud

Clearly, the now of nature is overshadowed as never before by an unsettling urgency concerning possible futures. As a poet, I sense this pressure at my shoulder and find it impossible in my poems to avoid or ignore the spreading cracks in our little terrarium. My usual entry into a poem is through the gateway of narrative—how things feel as they are experienced, in full knowledge and sometimes inclusion of shadowy signs. In some poems I may be in my own backyard, in others engaged in active imagination on a larger scale. But from my side of the opus, each poem is a meditation at play with microcosm and macrocosm, the day and the aeon. Nature's settings—cracks and all—encourage this kind of reflection in me, just by my standing still, quiet, in the glade of memory and imagination.

On a more transcendental level, as with Rilke and Jung and Teilhard de Chardin, I believe it is god, or the god image, that needs our knowledge, experience, and attention right now, to be born into what is needed next. One only needs to open a newspaper to be reminded of that. To me, this means dealing with one's own inherited *imago*—the god question—in terms of personal discoveries, early and late. Some of my poems enter this territory; but the task is not a matter of simply un-gilding the lily and viewing the rot as well. No "Howl" will do. Just ask Job. Thus, both the dark and the light aspects of god/nature enter into my poems, combining to form my best present feel for what the image wants in terms of completion and newly-stated consciousness.

Which is to say, I come to nature prepackaged with views and beliefs. I am not simply a camera receiving images passively and handing back random glossies. In my poems, I select for a world continuing into beauty and meaning, not for denial or apocalypse. I select images and vignettes—or, rather, they select me—that mix with my desire to find a way toward healing and advance, both for myself and for the world.

VOYAGEURS

A canoe trip for boys,
dropped off in base camp
up north above Lake Superior,
where we were bound to find Jesus,
twelve and a mild bearded guide.

Off we paddled
and down dark portage paths trudged
with our burdens, willowy backs bent
under packs and canoes and pup tents.

Lake after lake, each a steppingstone
on the looping quest, our prows pushing,
stick arms driving through each day's arc
marked in remorseless red
on a flat thumb-smeared map.

And it's days in and black night
around a dying confessional campfire,
our muttered fragments of witness
going smothered into the infinite woods,

when an arm shoots up, a call, rocking
all eyes north to aurora borealis, the sky
afire in a tide of cosmic lava, rising up
high, huge, gently—a temple
over our first felt solitude.

CONFIRMATION CLASS

The two-mile walk from school—half of it
along River Road—was more or less a mosey
in the general direction of Jesus. Being let out early,
going my own way alone—that was the main thing.

The gorge of the Mississippi was deep just there,
banks nearly sheer, the underbrush starving
beneath tall trees stretching for the sun
like overbalanced, half-toppling charismatics.

One elder ash tree put out a long telescoping
catwalk, proud as a pulpit over the abyss.
High in the treetop balcony, solid, it beckoned me
off the path, and every Wednesday I climbed

out to my pew and sat looking at the slow
river through a leafy rood-screen dapple.
My thighs hugged that old rugged bark, faith far off
in a chill church basement, my truancy a confirmation.

ANIMA MUNDI:
Four Possible Paintings

Shadowy behind her shoulder
red black storms churn and boil,
lifting up eons of debris,
a world crush of toppled
perfect bricks and fallen walls
of glass, that scavengers move through,
stooping to sort them back.

Far off, far beyond her call,
patriarchs clutch before a wall
with a stunted key,
one outstanding tooth
turning round and round,
never solving the lock.

Then quiet, murmuring
in no one's ear,
she stands up, leans
over the continent,
watching fenced fields
bleed into each other,
trees walk down the mountains
and across the plains.

Across scattered sunlight
a wolf pup pounces,
rolls onto its back,
playing, hugging
the bleached flute of a found rib.

A NATURE POEM

Summer assails the house
flooding the windows with green
with that feverish reaching
of trees and bush
over swollen turf
that crowds into every pane
like a sweaty mob
barely held back

And here
from the cave shade in the kitchen
the garage wall is hard to look at
its frieze of glare ruining the eyes
for the dishes
soaking in the sink
clubbing into each other
mindlessly
like icebergs
as I trouble the suds
testing for tepid

Close the eyes
Rest the senses for a moment
Walk soap-handed to the living room—
another window
cars slinking by
returning crazed glances
flung by the sun

And deep within the pane
the ice caps
like butter pats
slipping into liquid

BAD BOY
for Randy

At the park,
at maximum gallop,
flop ears flying
toward the dense grove opposite—

there, he's in beyond the sumac verge,
nosing the shadows
under a solemn old oak—

the layered archaeology of odors,
something like sociology in a clump of crow-
dropped squirrel fur, a quiz of seeds, turd stuff,
feather floss, whole histories of the vandal ants
and moth-winged martyrdoms, theology
in a shrugged cocoon, the architecture
of bark, clear genealogies of piss—

he droops his scholarly lip over every spoor,
stain, and carapace, meditating at length,
musing over each find, a savant over his text,
until a thick hand catches his clerical collar.

TWO CURRENT VERSIONS

1.

In the marginalia past sixty, October sun glares
off the back fence pickets, brief but blinding,
like a chide for lost higher angles and the upright middle,
as the still-clinging morning glories tip their faces
almost up at the bur oak puzzles overhead.

Another decade of summers gone, and it becomes
plausible, easy, to nod off into puttering, stoking
the fire slowly with foreshortened musings, to slump
like those fiddleheads going slowly brown, buckling,
barely standing up, first to be wrecked by frost.

2.

Last May I was sure I loved summer, the gradient sun
angling dome high, a million green pennants roused
from rootstock, affluent, bloom-proud, a quick colorful
paintbrush daubing away long views into difficult infinities,
the crowding annuals unafraid of shallow footing.

But now, with leaves all fallen, I can see much farther,
the spines and bones of things clear, pierceable
through and behind—that green ash made naked
for sun to find the window, the interior room, a potted
ten-year-old peace lily, alert on its trivet, gift when father went.

Lisa Ann Berg

I am grateful to write while being held by nature: the nature that surrounds, the nature that abounds, the nature that adapts, the nature that is beautiful and not beautiful;

the nature that gives rise to all of us and all that we create... the nature that lives beyond us and despite us.

I am grateful.

SMALL LAMENT, MIDSUMMER

I know, I know, there is no going back.

Especially when desire
for an old fullness
belongs to someone else's dream,
there is no revisiting that wish in my wish.

Instead, in the close heat,
the smell of wild roses
drenches me in sweetness

and occasionally I love my common history
and yearn now for a story in fragrance,

the marigolds, the sweet peas, the rain-soaked sidewalk.

SMALL IDYLL

and this July night

cool,

not quite like summer,

I saw

out
a way

from our small cities

fox
raccoon
owl
eagle
hawk
deer

...mostly though,

what came through me:

the smells of
wood burning,
dirt,
of decay,
growing corn,
of hay—

the world does
what the world does...

For now, I feel tethered   (don't you?)
to its movement,
its generous heart;
—this able,
generous heart,
its lushness
beyond us,
with us,
each day;
beyond us,
each day.

HERE NOW

the early fall can snap anyone
into the ripe and changing present;

this odd confluence of witnessed seasons:
dead spring lilacs still on their branches,
the remaining green of summer,
the movement of the rest:
the animals, the birds, the odd humans...

the movement toward, well,
winter;

though I think,
today,
it just might be good

to take in
early autumn,

to take a walk, call a friend,
rejoice a little
in
this day.

THIS DAY

There is no need to surrender
    each day
        to grief
for the world.

Somewhere in the Bible
it says that
creation waits with eager longing

We are part of creation, too
and long
and move

toward wholeness
or
hope.

We could surrender
to this day,

to this day.

SMALL REDEMPTION

    and on this day
when the thought came to me   (oddly)

that I was wrestling with wily demons;

when I couldn't
and wouldn't think

love
and
self

in the same sentence;

this day,

I tripped and slipped and fell
face down onto the cool grass.

The smell of dirt
and
green

(oddly)   a temporary *and* infinite balm;

enough.

I could trust, this day
    hope

the fecund earth.

THE WAITING

Sometimes,
the breeze
would be a reassurance.

More often though,
the blackened sky would come
thrumming toward them,
it could be hail or incredible rains,
approaching gradually
from a great seeable distance;
something to flatten
all evidence of their labor,
to take what they had to have.

This is
how waiting for disaster began,

seeing it come,
then understanding;
the helplessness,
then the waiting.

Suzanne Swanson

I'm not a nature writer. It's not how I see myself, anyway. The natural world—beautiful or not—is simply my base, what feeds me. I need art, I need the made thing, but without the rawest of raw materials—the earth, its food, its landscapes, our bodies, our births & deaths—and paying attention to how I respond to those materials, I languish. Plenty of my writing begins with the natural world, the stuff of the senses as the touchstone or stepping-off point. I often work fairly straightforwardly; I use metaphor less than many poets. I hope then that the words, forms, and juxtapositions I settle on will create a sensory impression that evokes each reader's personal experience of "like" or "is." I want the reader to compare my phrase, my poem, to the world she knows, its concrete/natural building blocks, its transcendent moments or patterns—not deliberately, but evocatively.

And do I love this faltering earth? Yes, I love this earth.

plain

a meadowlark abides the fence, the plains—
the woman, grown, recalls that burbled song
running like water flows where there is none.
not *none* but *lack* her sense, the base,

a landscape made for living things who base
their hearts in *just enough*, no need past one
small stand of cottonwoods, calm guards along
a cracked creekbed, filled by her bird's refrain

1981, 2008

The summer you were born
Spring had breathed slow
Into fullness, colors each by each
In turn as the buds unfurled.

Spring, I breathed slow,
You under my ribs,
A bud unfurling,
Filling our air with expectation.

You, under my ribs,
Grew my belly broad and wide.
I filled with expectation,
Surprised at passion's steady pace.

My belly, broad, wide,
Held your world, pink and lush.
Surprised at passion's steadying pace
I watched the earthly seasons turn.

I was your world—you pink, lush,
All becoming: branch, leaf, petal.
I watched you turn and turn
In my body, sensed ripening:

Tender leaf and petal into fruit.
Finally ready, you came to us, July's prize.
In my ripening body, I'd sensed
Yours, opening me. Leaving me.

You arrived, July's prize,
Mid-summer you were born.
Your body, opening mine, left me
For further fullness, summer's deepening colors.

BEACH 4

a whirring in the mind
against nature's roar
the ongoingness

how a wave appears
to make itself, that
a wave is enslaved, tethered

to weather barely
able to be plotted   she has
outwaited the lack of sea-

stars, now their orange
peeks from the water-
line, emerges from the twice-

night darkness
of water. there is
a strength in remainder.

if the ones she loves
were here, they could
make her happy, pull out

the names of every one
of these gulls
yes / no   she has

carried them   belly and back
along and she does not
need to know

BEST GUESS

Their islands will disappear
in sixty years. Will
    be gone. For a time
    the corrugated tin hats
of the houses will act
as if they are floating
    on the ocean. The ocean
    will no longer distinguish itself
from the lagoon. *Ni* and *wyni*
will become identical in their non-
    existence, no longer new coconut
    and mature, gifts of God. The roots
of those palms will pickle
in brine. Under their stalks /how long
    will they stand—bent, bowing—
    in the Pacific?/ waves ~
under the waves, a perfect
home for leopard-skin
    shells like the one Lino, loving
    his lagoon—knowing it—wrapped
into my surprised hand, his face
dripping from the dive, vision
    direct but dimmed behind the mask.

DEATH TRIES TO TEACH HER

Yesterday the nuthatch pair advantaged themselves
of the silver maple, angle after angle. Their orientation
is their own. Gravity can be rethought

at every degree of the compass. She's made
that shaky alliance with grief and distance. Ambidextrous
toward both, yet she does not recall

how to decide which hand to extend first. And
she can't seem to forget "upright." In ways she never needed
to imagine, she was anchored to her mother. Has to

see it now via contrast—cut free, a floater, all the footings
refigured. Stares out the window at the maple's feathered
trunk, watches the nuthatches claim it as they will.

SOME DAYS

You wish never to leave this earth. The weight

of body on body, the pushing of mower and stroller,

the heart's beating along its private and collective

spectrum: terror, anger, joy, expectation. Today,

the opening of the seams of the body into heron-green

water below the surface blue.

Mary Junge

Knowing with the head is not enough. One must know some things with the bones.
    Danilo Dolci, Sicily

If our imperiled earth is to be saved, it will be saved, I believe, by our hearts rather than by our heads. We already know that our civilization must make radical changes in order to stop global warming, yet we are not racing to make those changes. Knowledge, unfortunately, takes us only part of the way to a solution. We will change, eventually, because of love, when we finally conclude that we love the earth, ourselves, and our children and grandchildren enough—when we acknowledge that *we* are of the earth in the same way that a tree or flower is of the earth. Before love comes deep knowledge—the kind we carry in our bones. Adults generally do not take the time necessary to study nature, to look carefully at the *small beauties*.

The images of the natural world are seeded in us in childhood—as we sit around campfires weaving Indian grass, or on the beach while witnessing turtles hatching and then scurrying into the dangerous waters (where half die), or walking in woods and eating berries straight off the bush. The prairies of North Dakota and the lakes of northern Minnesota formed and informed me, and their images still color my vision. I am made of them just as I am made of muscle, bone, and skin.

The prairie is magnificently diverse and may change according to the light and weather. A field hosts hues of white, tan, brown, yellow, green, blue—and seem iridescent in the right light. Some days the wind gives sound to the fields as it shakes the tassels or whistles through the grasses. Within the field grasses, or in a partly sunny part of a wooded area, delicate flowers hide, our orchid-like ladyslipper, for instance, which requires the shade of other plants. The ladyslipper takes her time: up to sixteen years to produce her first flower, and the plant is so delicate that attempts at transplantation usually result in death, a serious matter given that these plants are endangered and, if not disturbed, can live up to fifty years.

How will we learn to resist the temptation to transplant and change, and instead learn to live as part of the existing natural world? Can we learn to walk lightly among the small beauties? Will we find a way to marry ourselves to nature before it is too late to save our home?

THE WATER CARRIED

In tall, clear drinking glasses, to sick children. In the uterus, without much thought of it. In plastic bottles, over oceans, fearing thirst. In dreams, to those dying in the desert: 70% of the earth is water, but no water. In rain catchers, astonished. In the mouth during a rainstorm, ecstatic. In a small corked tube, to an altar, Lourdes. In a dog's dish, to the dog waiting in the car. To restaurant tables, four and five glasses at a time. In a pitcher, to the family dinner table. With hose and sprinkler, to the browning grass. In the mouth, head tilted back, ecstatic. In a carafe, to droopy houseplants. In a cup, to the pan of rice. In cupped hands, to wet the head, cool the body. In cupped hands, to douse a fire. In cupped hands, to the mouth. In a thimble. In a thimble. In a thimble, because there was no cup. In pails, from the lake to the sandcastle's moat. In pails, to add cool water, hot sand beach, New Zealand. In a jug, from a stranger's hands, lifted to the mouth, a ready O, Grand Canyon. To the porcelain tub for baby's bath, slippery and most precious fruit. From the bucket to the pan for warming feet—to warm the body. To the teapot, then cup, to the waiting mouth, the grateful body—the body, more than half water.

GIRL PUTTING AWAY THE LILY POND FOR WINTER
Como Conservatory, St. Paul, Minnesota

Because I am a grandmother, and because it seems like I should know something about the huge lily pads before us, I make something up: *She is putting away the lily pond for the winter*, I say in my most authoritative voice. One thing I know for sure: this girl has found her calling. She loves water lilies—it's obvious in the graceful way she moves through the water in her waders, her inner music set to the slowest speed. We stand with the gathering crowd at the edge of the pond. She is oblivious to us as she stacks the pads, which look like huge green paper party bowls, their edges folded upward so perfectly to keep them afloat. The girl sets them on the growing pile on the cart beside the pool, and each one makes a dry sound when added to the stack, telling us of their lightness, but also reminding us that they are oh so temporary—not unlike ourselves—and will soon be turned back to the earth. This reminds us that winter is coming, and we are not quite ready for it, so we stand and stare, as if time has no beginning or end, at the girl moving slowly among the lily pads. She stacks a few pads, snips underwater for awhile, then brings up a small green bundle. Now that I have lost my will to be an authority any longer, we stand together quietly, watching the mermaid-like girl as she wades among the lily pads in the dark waters. I think of Ella's future and wish for her this kind of happiness—or whatever it is I am seeing in this tall girl tending the water lilies.

MOUNT RAINIER, 2008

As we ascend in rain,
Slower for our age and the thin air,
The young ones pass in their red and yellow
Hooded rain jackets.

Up to the marmots at the waterfall,
The gray jays at the scenic lookout,
The fearless grouse, and finally the gray glaciers.
How little the rain dampens our spirits,

The mountain stands like a house of love. Rain,
Beautiful rain
Reminds of our wilderness honeymoon
Thirty-two years ago—

The power of a sudden wall of water, Canada.
This rain falls gently, caressing the mountain
Ever so slowly.
With youth goes impatience.

On a pile of gray rocks a single pink flower stands tall,
A tiny spot of color.
You can see love in any good heart the same
As you can see the snow-capped mountain peaks

Through the veil of rain and fog.

LAST NIGHT

Saved a pink ladyslipper,
Caught the thief with shovel in hand,
About to lift roots and all,
Her children waiting in the car.

Saved a ladyslipper from the quick death
That comes after transplantation
From its hiding place, where hosta leaves shade
Its flowers, sixteen years coming.

Saved a showy ladyslipper
While our good earth seems to be slipping away—
To poachers resembling ourselves—
The glow of our wonderment shadowed by our greed.

DEDICATION, DARWIN DAY, 2009

To search for something simple and true,
Some small beauty in the middle of a gray day
In February, grass pushed up around patches of snow.
To register the houses in Minneapolis and
Across the country, empty now, dark and vacant.
To look for something beyond this day—
Beyond the hawk, dead on the freeway.
To imagine Darwin in his next life
Taking in music and poetry every week, knowing
The loss of these is a loss of happiness…

To puzzle over how we use camouflage, fabric of
Hunters and warriors, to make fashion,
Skirts and everyday pants—even diaper bags.
To call them mine, those who send dear ones to Iraq,
And also the young ones who think they must go.
To praise the human will to decide anything.

To Darwin who loved slow turtles.
To the baby turtles I watched as a girl,
Battling the waves of Big Floyd Lake.
To natural selection,
To revising theories and plans.
To accidents and errors. To penicillin.
To the evolution of our species,
To what we could become.
To what we will become.
To the busy spiders in the vacant houses.
To hope, especially, and always:
To hope.

Note: "If I had to live my life again, I would have made a rule to read some
poetry and listen to some music at least once every week; for perhaps the parts

of my brain now atrophied would thus have been kept active through use. The loss of these tastes is a loss of happiness, and may possibly be injurious to the intellect, and more probably to the moral character, by enfeebling the emotional part of our nature." From *Charles Darwin's Autobiography*, New York: Henry Schulman Inc., 1950, pg. 67.

THE PASSAGE

The newborn's eyes shift to follow
Motion in the woods.
Here, the deer have been assigned nothing less than
Death—for eating tulips and denting cars.
Like my new granddaughter, my head today seems
Too heavy for my neck.

What would a bird do with worry?
Drop it in flight?
Use it as lining for the nest?
Leave it, a trap, for predators.
As if we could always go forward.
As if anyone has ever known a repair for ruin,
As if we could see where the great owl goes
After it flies over, then on,
Into the blackness of the night.

Margot Fortunato Galt

Some poets stitch nature into us—Gerard Manley Hopkins's thrumming language brings poplars alive, even as he mourns their destruction. Greeks and other stargazers stamp the heavens with human myth. Does this matter to the stars? There are humans who believe their actions bring qualities in the earth alive—Bruce Chatwin's *Songlines* describes Australian aborigines compelled to walk life into the landscape of their story songs. Afrikaner Laurens van der Post tracks the oldest African humans, the Bushmen, and finds that, for them, the European presence robs ancient sites of their power. There must be ways we can draw closer and listen to sustaining nature. Lately, I'm trying to pare away the ego, become as transparent as possible, and "conduct words" with white space, to slow down and let us ponder.

From "Prairie—Seven Poems for Photographer Linda Gammell"
SHE WANTED

to record
only one small
portion, one bird,
one snake, one
unc fly's view.

Nothing grand
one blade, one stem,
one pistil at a time

as if creation
commenced
in a haze
of exasperated
jerks.

She arrived
three days early
to scope out
the spot

deciding
where to plant
herself, where

to start

the slow
   erasure

the wearing in.

SHE MEANT

not to insist,

her extra eye
low to the ground
girdling two
rose hips

while a third,
lower, catches
warmth
at its crown

and two more
burst in the dark.

She meant
to look so long
she stopped
believing

she had ever
been new

now part
of the day

the light
the half-knowing.

The rest
in blurred shadow
belongs

to some
other

in sight.

PRAIRIE ROSE HIPS: AUTUMN

Morning opens its mouth
on a haze of pleasure
ready to swallow
that thieving night,
its dreams.

COMMON MULLEIN

It could not be
more phallic.
She's heard of barbs
studding the members
of some male animals.
But this,
this thrust
of rough seeds
into womb of sky,
this brings down
the sun.

summer drives

silences
        on the road past the boy scout camp
the lake on one side
                grey blue
summer homes on the other
       wide lawns   windmills   gourds for birds

gravel crunching under the tires

I remember none of your words
on the drive to the dump
                      bottles smashed
white refrigerators with their doors off

did I mention huge pines
fronting a farm house before the road curved
                              wild roses
growing from the mow of a barn

comfortable or anxious
                watching the signs
green fields   brown fields   the one stop
where we turned left
                we were coming closer
your hands on the wheel
                your profile to my turned face
my thoughts flowing speechless
                      over the landscape

LAKE DROUGHT

Even on these rocks
scum, often under water

whitens in the sun.
The lake lowers
another notch.

Burn off, disaster.
This is August,

common spoke on
the wheel to ice.

Praise heat, our
night will come.

The king makes his
rounds, never blinks.

But only if
we had stayed put,

stopped migration
in flaming cars,

not torched trees
to match the sun.

Each decade sloughed
faster, snake skin
of our greed.

Now to wait
on dumb rocks,
their grey flanks
patient to the end,

come home, hands
filled with empty
bottles, cans,

    late bouquet
of small worries.

Su Smallen

How does the natural world feed into my writing life? I have eddied with this question like a novitiate with a koan, a question without an answer, because what writing life would I have without the natural world? Our word *nature* comes from the Latin *natura* and *nasci*, to be born. To be born into the physical world and its phenomena: breath, ink and paper, image, symbol, synaptic transfer, electrochemical signal, vibrating superstring: meaning. In my yellow quilt in my yellow room in my grandparents' house among old trees in a town in a valley surrounded by farms and marshes and woods and roads in counties in climates in systems in clusters in galaxies, I am smaller than the living organisms inside me. Are we not earth, ocean, and air for what lives within us, what makes us live, in fact? All is one. Time exists, noted Einstein, so that everything doesn't happen at once. The divisions we make in our physical world, like minutes and weeks, like "the natural world" and "my life," we *make* so that we don't see, hear, smell, feel, sense everything at once, so that we can *do*. But this at-once-ness is our natural state. It happens, sometimes, that what I make and do falls away. I might be paddling in the Boundary Waters, or a bald eagle might fly over from the Mississippi to fish a small urban lake, or a storm might down our power lines, or pooling cool moonlight might wake me into suspension, into all-is-one, into everything-at-once. I feel this and know it to be my stillpoint, where I am in balance, where I am trued. I am in a state of wonder, a state of being in which I cannot integrate in the way I ordinarily do. I feel more myself. I might *respond* to this surplus being, to act in return, to give. One way I respond is to *write*: to compose, to form, to spell.

BELOVED IS LIKE A PERFECT DAY

                              A cathedral,

empty with things as they are, empty, with a mystery
no one trespasses. Big news moves to the periphery,

big questions also. Blown-out. The last lift
toward *toward*, /the interval/, the first fall toward—

when some arrangement solves. Our wanting does not change
anything. The day moves out of center, acuity

falls off, into the outermost, the field of movement
and ghostly shapes. Our bodies are made of living, with straps

for tumbling through all this, without being let go of.
Our bodies naturally stream and pour, yet we tire. Here

we have a small dam. We allow us to be diverted.
We must. At some point, our vigil must be relinquished.

The last weight of light tilts away. How do we
let go of perfect days? We love them. They go.

DEATH IS THE INNERMOST HUNTER

i.
As if absentmindedly smoothing and resmoothing the tablecloth,
    the wind
looks at her across the lake. Trying to find a way to say this so
    she understands.

ii.
Weary at noon, he would climb
from the basement entrance, up
the stairs, into the kitchen,

to the chair at the table
by the door. Eat pretty much
silently. Take his pocket

watch out from his bib overalls.
Breathe. Go back downstairs and out
through the basement door back to

the fields, the sheds, or the cow barn.
So many places she was not
allowed to follow him.

iii.
The spirit and the body
began their separation
long ago. She started to see:

This is his body. This is him.
She noticed it as conflict.

iv.
The not-breath lengthens, suspends
As the breath shallows
His mouth open, as if singing

v.
To be free of a disintegrating body! Yet
the beauty of today. Green sparkling white pine in blue.
Small orange leaves that the maple hangs onto, for her.

vi.
He didn't seem to need anything.
I don't need anything, he always said.

vii.
I'll see you later:
she has—we all have—

dedicated neurons.
She has assigned hers

to him so she will
recognize him

when she sees him
from a new angle.

viii.
Small revelations: *I never
used to like milk*, he said one day.
He had been a dairy farmer.

ix.
How breath leaves.
The last one, she thinks it was
the last, so small.
Like in-breathing the word
oh

x.
His palm where it had lain on his diaphragm.
At the source of last breath, his palm was sweaty.

xi.
Driving so fast,
county roads, hills
and curves—she felt
the earth like braille.
When she lies down,
her sensation
replays it all:
she is again
in the dark
up down around
faster than she
dares signs jumping
up lights sweeping
hills fields curves:
The earth she feels
is a body.

xii.
She can not garden
this year, she has had enough

death, she can not pull
steadfast grass, optimistic
saplings, Dickinson's clover.

xiii.
Dances on Tuesdays,
walk through the corn on Sundays.
We had fun.
Well, I think that's about it.

BUDDHA, EGRET

The Great Egret, too

Luminous in the twilight

Trespassing the spirit state

She stands where she has never

Stood, fishes from there

SNOW THAT FALLS LIKE AMNESIA

For the big nouns/truth, faith, trust, love/all her images have been stripped/She can't recall /everywhere lies crystalline sundials/She can't recall every/where lies/She bundles up, goes walking in statistics, disinterest, reversals/Can only think she once thought this: beauty/If she kept walk/ing kept/walking/kept walk/ing until she slept/a snow mummy who/when found /would only be remembered for being found/in snow/perfect/as if/she would open her eyes and speak/were she not shattered/What image now /can she claim? This evidence/small animals tracking among the stones/The field beyond indicated by an absence of trees/Or the graves themselves/her new lake to walk around/the world on her left/death on her right/or/an image of death/The snow/like a calm hand/stays the clock hands of the dewy dead

>—with gratitude to Patricia Weaver Francisco
> and Deborah Keenan

NOVEMBER 3, 2004 / WHAT PREVAILS

Though last night's grins were eaten out of pumpkins
And conditions suggested a killing frost,

Some pariahs were embraced. The grief that holds
While it happens is different than the let-go

Grief that in the open doorway encloses.
Unlike law, in love there is no exit.

And pariahs, born to the border life, will
Slip limits. Today it is warm enough

To raise from the neglected litter one
Leaf. Look, it's a monarch. Call her Ruth.

KINDS OF SNOW

> *Can you punctuate yourself as silence? You will see the edges cut away from you, back into a world of another kind—back into real emptiness, some would say. Well, we are objects in a wind that stopped, is my view.* —Anne Carson, Plainwater

3a. *Sparrow Snow*
Snow jumps like sparrows from the middle of the arborvitae to its edges, appearing whole out of disappearance. Our eyes are too slow to see the continuity of sparrows. They jump or spring from the bush to the feeder—where does this coil reside in them? Then from the feeder back to the bush. Their language we call song because we don't understand its poetry, its prosody, its litany of kinds of shadows. We take it as a mythology of joy.

7a. *Snow of the Fields*
The snow of the fields this year is sparse. A tweed of snow, dirt, and corn stubble. Another farm sold. A quick creep of houses.

11. *Snow that Reminds Me of My Mother*
This tumble of oranges in the grocery store
in November, she recalls her San Diego
wedding, the orange blossoms

13c. *Breaking Snow*
Walk with a wider stance, with gravity surely landing each step, with the confidence of a Cooper's hawk pitched at a hundred sparrow wing beats into arborvitae.

15a. *Blue Moon Snow*
There is snow that comes in bulk, and brings silence, because it stops us. This hour we wouldn't otherwise be given, a discontinuity in our industry, a mended film, with many frames missing.

15b. *Negative Snow*

A mended film, with many frames missing. A leap of faith of narrative, of flight from dark to bright to dark. The shadow overhead returning from the highest tree.

16. *The Snow that Burns in My High Heart, after Sending Sparrows Out of My Body*

Our high heart is where our left hand rests when we curl into fetal position. If, as we uncurl, we let our left palm turn over, to press our opening chest, we are now touching ourselves as we do when taken aback. A part of our souls would jump out if we did not hold ourselves there. But gravity's just a slipknot, and souls sometimes send themselves away, home, safe. The shaman retrieves them, blows them back into our high hearts.

17. *Snow of Short-Term Memory Loss*

Is it snowing? yes.
Is it snowing? yes. It is snowing.
Is it snowing? yes. It is still snowing.
Is it snowing? yes. It snows all day.

19b. *Snow that Falls from Books*

If you turn the page from the corner, it can sound like walking in snow.

19c. *Rising Snow*

Snow rises at the heat of the window like joy.

22. *Snow that Reminds of the Dying Dog*

We no longer know whose life we are praying for
It is late April and the daffodils are budding

25c. *Snow of the Calendar*

All the little marks.
Dictators.

29a, b. *The Snow that Attaches,*
The snow that falls away.

32. *Other Kinds of Snow*
There is snow that falls separate from the sky, and snow that is the sky itself falling, the sky itself reaching down to us (not falling). This is confusing. What does it mean to become lost? Sparrows need carry no marrow, only air. They move easily within this truth. The truth being that brilliance is all there is. The rest we make.

Annie Breitenbucher

For me, the impulse to write connects with the experience of being "cracked open"—being totally, even uncomfortably alive. I've had this experience hiking in the Rocky Mountains, running down Summit Avenue on a warm December day, playing softball on a perfect summer night. In these moments, when my small life intersects with the natural world, I'm left with a profound sense of restlessness. There is urgency, the fierce desire to elevate my game: to do it right, live well, journey honestly.

MY FATHER AT SUNSET

Tonight
Last night
The nights before—
Around this corner
a bend of light through tall
grass and flowers planted wild.

All the colors of sunset: Lemon, melon,
cherry, received by the rims, the spokes, the blue
bike frame and—finally—me. Me receiving
the particles that must be you. Light
confetti in my nose, my throat, and

Filling my chest with that
bittersweet sorrow:
Having you here,
then not. Always
I am taken by
surprise.

THIS IS MY STORY

It burned inside
of me until
I could carve it
into the land.
Sometimes
I needed to mark
my way—return
to what was known.
Sometimes
I celebrated the hunt,
the sky, the mystery
of abundant rain.
Sometimes
I mourned
what was lost.
I am among
the vanished ones.
And still
my story lives on.

It burns inside
while I look for
rock and knife.
Sometimes
I need to see
my path.
Sometimes
I need to celebrate
the walk, the bounty,
the mystery: How
lucky am I?
Sometimes
I need to mourn
what I am not.
I am among
the vanishing ones
searching for signs
before my story
is lost.

Note: The petroglyphs above were photographed at White Tank Mountain Regional Park in southern Arizona. They are believed to be the work of a people known as the Hohokam, who settled there from approximately 300 BC to 1500 AD, when their culture inexplicably vanished. Hohokam means the "vanished ones."

Last ride

late November.
Leaves gone,
wind scouring
heat from
the sun.

Bright sun
filleting the chest
like a diamond-edged
knife. Clean cut
no sound.

No sound
on the lake—
just the radio.
The music in my head
lapping side-to-side
ear-to-ear.
Movement—

Gear to gear
Heart to legs
Legs to pedals
Pedals to wheels.

—A star, a song, a bike—
reaching over
the carnivorous dark.

BEAUTIFUL
For Mary

Out on the water the sun has gone,
the sparkling wetness turned dark, murky brown.

Out on the water the rain starts soft,
leaves cool bubbles on our skin as we

cast with no sound but the line spinning out,
tumbling down, coming back in that rhythm of retrieval.

In this water, in this boat, my sister and I cast
side-by-side and do not consider

the fish as much as the air: the cool, wet air
breaking us open. Mary and I in the rhythm of no sun,

Mary and I repeating, cast after cast,
Isn't it beautiful?

PAIRED

Three little white whiskers
A blush of gray in tiny black paws

A thousand routines we have settled into,
like an old married couple

journeying against the grain of time:
getting it right, and not.

I watch you now
asleep in my lap—

your fur moving softly
up and down and

behold the hand of a Matchmaker,
with all the blessings and heartaches
that pairings require.

THE SUN SITS DOWN

So much fatigue.
24 hours, 365 days of rotating,
and the sun sits down—
spreads arms, legs, rays
in the cool mountain stream.

It surveys its work:
tall grass bleached brittle and white.
It feels the thirsty roots
reach for water.

It does what it was meant to do:
spin and throw
heat and light.
Even now, exhaling waves
of yellow and red that
ripple downstream.

Soon it will gather itself,
head west;
too tired at day's end
to be seen.

Millions of years—
same route, same job and always
too much or
not enough.

Nancy Walden

A clear, cold night in October—the sky loaded with stars, the Milky Way bold and white. Sleep, and then the morning's blue skies, and the delight of a fresh snowfall that snuck in sometime between the clarities of midnight and dawn. We can't schedule delight, and are simply the poorer for ignoring it. This is what matters, right here, right now: the clear air, the bright maple leaves sailing down with pats of snow hitching rides on their shoulders, the deer tracks leading out of the marsh.

At our best, humans are mindful of the parts we can play in stopping the wreckage of the world by other humans, and we act on that awareness. As poets, we hope to inspire others to look and feel and to act to protect our environment.

Right now, I lay my words down like leaves along that maple branch, accept the snow, and delight in the breeze that carries me on.

BOUNDARY WATERS

paddling by
twisted roots
restless young tree pulls away
from all that holds him

we canoe,
hot summer day
black and orange butterfly floats,
floats

tiny toad on
a warmed granite boulder
absorbs this,
just this

WHITE

Three brides on every branch
Grand bouquets of being
White nuptial plumes

Egrets in tropical trees
Airy

HUMMINGBIRD

As you flash by, I understand that we see almost everything differently. But, we both arrived at the same summering place, and I'm trying to envision how you left the Yucatan Peninsula, flew across the Gulf of Mexico in twenty-six hours without a stop, and returned safely to the very spot you left last fall. You follow no other hummingbird, insist on flying alone, and you are so irascible! Do the stars help you find focus, does the magnetic field direct your mind? I understand what it's like to follow a train of thought. Is that the sensation? Like following a faint, blue thread?

MAP AND DRUM

—then I
tiptoed across a rollercoaster road
and into the consciousness of a small place

Here is my map, an X marking a certain tall poplar tree,
curiously alive,
pocked by a pair of pileated woodpeckers

one drums on a hollow tree nearby

Silently now,
my leaf-covered path intersects
with that of a great Blanding's turtle

Intrigued, alert, we eye one another,   cock our heads,
each feeling (I would guess)   a bit far afield—

HUMPBACK WHALE

how wild and strange
is your sudden appearance,
blasting open the doors between our lives
with a noisy exhalation of breath and ocean spray

my first glimpse of your strong, curved back
and the white birthmarks of your mottled tail

now you've disappeared into the silkiness
of the ocean depths

around my boat, the water still vibrates
with long waves and circles
a moving, visible thrill

little time together
just pleasure,
and my attempt, in friendship,
to call you back

SANDHILL CRANE

    We call you
    the Great Bird of Happiness
It is not your voice so much
as the call and response
between you and your mate
that brings us joy.
    Can you hear me?
        Yes, I hear you.
    Are you near?
        Yes, I'm near.
    Will you stay?
        Yes, I'll stay.
Caught up in your optimism and grace,
We mimic and jump and spread our arms wide
And then one day, you answer the urge to disappear into the tundra,
choosing a place at the very fringe of the possible
to rear your young.
We wonder,
    Will you survive?
    Yes, as for the past 60 million years, we'll survive.

Ann Iverson

The natural world is a window. We thrust it open, air out stagnant thoughts, let go of the ordinary. The winds of imagination roll in.

Imagination fills the empty page, and while these words might not save the natural world, they save us. The eagle, gliding through a transparent sky, calms. The tortoise plodding without rush slows us. The cat cleaning his mane makes us responsible to ourselves. Birds on the wire, in October snow, make us durable. Leaves wanting to be orange provide the wherewithal for us to become who we need to be in all the goodness and despair, in all the light and dark.

RECKLESS

In every heart there is
a reckless summon
calling us
from ordinary
delivering us
from order
saving us
from certainty.

Is there a problem
with chaos?

Look at the daisies
along the bay,
scattered haphazard
for a good stretch of mile,
like hippies at a sit down.

One week they are there.
The next, gone.

Who would mow down
this mob?

Who would
thrash the principle?

All of us need more often
to turn up wild in a field.

ALL THESE BUTTERFLIES

About happiness,
they are never wrong

as one seemed
to love me all day long

as I worked the lonesome
acres of this land.

Perhaps my sweat
was the attraction

as it kept landing
on my shoulder

darting towards
my heart

twinkling
with desire.

The plunge and readiness
for nectar, the succulent

bead on the
heat of my skin,

mistaken for
hibiscus.

Of evasion, they are genius.
Congregation too, a multiplicity

of both worlds, the introvert,
the extrovert.

Explaining why all of them
didn't flutter up and follow.

And in some world, I thought
that I deserved that.

THE GREAT BLUE HERON

I love
the Great Blue Heron
nesting on the pond.

I love his stress
when the red-winged
black birds

peck at his head
with retribution
for egg thievery

I love how
he stands up and
takes it all

the swirling wings
of tiny payback
and I love

how the day exists
beneath his wings
and even more

how they unfold:
feather to muscle to bone
to flight and to somehow

I matter
not
in any of it.

DAY LILY AND THE SPARROW

While the lily has seven tongues
She has nothing to say

To make the bird work harder.
Flitter, flutter, fetch and tote.

Like a woman carrying
A basket on her head.

The work is never done.
The decisions never made.

~

If I could put my tongue to yellow
I might feel absolute

Or place my palm on the underside
Of one white feather.

A faithful gray squirrel
Darts up through the elms;

A pink patch of Wednesday
Bleeds from the sun.

The sky is one palette today
The earth is another.

How will I do my work?
What does the lily have to say?

HER JOB AT DUSK WHILE A STORM THREATENS

The earth gathers what she can:
Rabbit, doe, turkey, pheasant,
Mallard, birch, sand, pine, and fox.

Lets go of clover and tulip,
of oak, weasel, cattail,
the brown-eyed conundrum of forest,
the murky complacency
of water.

Picks up, as she flees,
crickets one by one.
Sweeps up the dull
center of mud.
Tucks in the corners
of uprooted elm.

Devours petunia,
daisy, not the rose,
no never the rose,
snake and fire.
So thirsty, swallows the pond
in one gulp.

Wants to steal lark,
finch, blue jay, rainbow,
shadows of oak pressed
against the sky.

TO KNOW A SNOW ANGEL

Is to love

what will wash away

with the wind

and drifted days.

Her wings will fade

so gently

into the blanched sky.

Deer might come

to see

what has dissolved.

There are no lights

on a distant tree,

no sleigh bells.

No ringing of anything

anywhere.

Nolan Zavoral

The truth is, I can't compartmentalize the natural world, hold it in a separate sphere and describe how it filters into my writing. The natural world is pervasive and pivotal, both in my work and in my being. I joke that I can't identify large numbers of flora and fauna, but that doesn't mean my heart doesn't sing in their presence.

INTRODUCTIONS

I could tell you about the bird singing in my backyard this morning. I could even play its half-note melody on the piano. Then you'd want to know the bird's name, and I would seize up. I don't know much about nature except it's here and so am I and sometimes that's enough. Take the tree in back insisting he'll live through winds and storms and advancing years, like me. Now, I know cottonwoods give off white fluff, and weeping willows slump over themselves, as if they've seen one too many office parties. But the tree out there is neither a cottonwood nor a weeping willow. What it is, I can't say. Sometimes after mowing or a walk I will stroke the old coot's bark. It knows me. I'd introduce you, but I'm bad with first names.

FUNKY LITTLE POEM

Take this funky little poem with you
into the woods and you will avoid
attacks by fanged fawns. Nature
will open, welcome you in.

If you need a friend, this funky little poem stands
ready. To it, you are light and love and your body
looks just right. To it, your lapses and your longings
make you most cherished.

Be kind: Tell this funky little poem jokes, beginning,
"So these two poets walk into a bar…" Feel these lines
grow warm on the page, behold their buckling into rainbows.
Let's see Billy Collins top that.

PETITION

Give me a brace of mornings like this one,
Bright and cool, blue sky, silence, my cat
Hunkered at the open window on my desk,
Crouched to make herself small should varmints
Appear. Once she leaped so hard at a rabbit
Hopping below on the grass that she stubbed
Her nose on the screen. Somehow it all seems
Of a piece, me, my cat, nature—skein of tranquility.
Yesterday a friend said she had agreed to look in
On a neighbor sinking into Alzheimer's
Abyss. The 63-year-old woman couldn't remember
The young girl in a photograph was her daughter.
I am 66. Me, my cat, nature. And a brace of
Mornings like this one.

JANE'S GARDEN
(For Jane Resh Thomas)

Maybe Luther Burbank could name the umpteen plants
and flowers occupying her backyard, but I can' t. Those dots of purple
cascading down the side of her house, a few feet from the front door. Or
the orange flowers broken open by their yellow lapping tongues. Peonies
I spot immediately, because we had a red corsage of them out the kitchen
window of my boyhood home. On the fringe of that yard stood three lilac bushes
whose brief fragrance passed through heaven on the way to your nose.
But here, in Jane' s garden, each week there is a newcomer working center stage
under an invisible baton. Not one scrap of grass can grow, so crowded is the space, yet
room enough for bugs and bees and Jane' s rascal mutt, Gilley. Sometimes the spectacle
forces you back a step, to inhale richness, to see the rooted rainbows bestowing their
colors on gardener and fool alike.

ONE DAY

One day newspapers will banner
"World Disarmament Begins."

Sea turtles will multiply furiously,
waddle inland, defecate in Crawford, Tex.

Cars will run on crushed cell phones.

We will learn to talk intelligently
to animals—they've waited for so long.

Especially cats.

66

I won't time myself today. I will let the lull of the freestyle lift me
Through this precious hour of my 66th birthday. The lanes are
Empty except for me. All I hear is the /clip-clip/ of my hands entering
Water, right-left, as sweet and serene as birdsong. The sound says:

You've nailed it, now ride the stroke. Swimmers want to slide through
Water on their sides, like a yawing sailboat, not bull straight-ahead like
A garbage scow. There's probably a metaphor for life in this, but it makes
Me think too hard.

Once, maybe, many birthdays ago. But that was during my Blue Period. My
Cat-less, Annie-less years. I flip-turn off a wall, reverse direction, /clip-clip/,
Still no one around to observe this marvel of 66-dom, this fleshy, fishy creature
Begoggled under a lime green cap. I am a seal, a dolphin, anything I want.

Eileen O'Toole

Today I'm thinking about how *earth* and *heart* are anagrams for one another, how they contain *ear* and *hear*, how *hearth*, a word that beautifully evokes home, encircles them all.

I'm thinking about curves and waves, what circles and what circulates—how everything relates and how central listening.

SUMMER, EARTH

What once was given—

Youth: an unfolding
view. Field of wheat-
gold lions—

—What was never given:

The ability to retrieve—

Splendor of any-
thing with words—

IN THE WAKE OF THE FLOOD WE PITCH OUR TENTS

Two generations of women
Who can read the signs:

Water lines on trees   Root River   detritus

We wade through dislocated dunes
To a bend where a river-trove of stones
Has been coughed up

Stones with holes
We string and weigh their mystery
Adorn ourselves as the sun goes down

Tribe of here we are

Beyond our fire eyes

CINQUE TERRE

We who sit at the sea's edge
        watch circling
                birds a shade darker than dusk.

Our bodies circling
        away from the sun
                though even now circling toward
        the sun consoled
and inconsolable.

        Vernazza's main road—
                we followed it
down to the western horizon
        to find the sun
                unadorned.

We watched it hover
        then slip
                memorized it

were evening mesmerized
        by waves, seamless
                displacement of light
                        by degrees, how
                darkness mutes a rocky shore.

Meanwhile earth pulls
                us close, rolls.

And as if it was
        what we were made for
                we watch
                        what disappears.

MONKEYS OF TAMBOPATA

Howler	Squirrel
sub-verbal pre-dawn	ear to canopy
roadless yogi	track lightning flock
breath and bellow prodigy	treetop gypsies
mountain exhaling	cloud gossip
left lung oracle	leaf activists
subterranean veils	sweep electric

Joyce Kennedy

Poetry usually conveys an intimacy with nature or with human nature. The two are close to being the same—we humans are, after all, part of nature, even though we now seem to be embedded in technology, nature farther and farther away from our urban environments of cement, freeways, and shopping malls. In my 4th floor perch in a city condo, I see a line of trees in the distance and I hear birds in the distance—sometimes I see them in flight. The clouds, though—great, moving, changing groups of them—have a presence in my life that hasn't been there since my days of growing up on the North Dakota prairie.

I feel that as a poet I have an obligation to maintain a watch on the increasing dangers to the earth and to its living creatures, including ourselves. Intimacy with nature is part of the poet's fieldwork. Nature provides text for what we do. Poetry that becomes increasingly detached from the natural world is in danger of becoming an abstract system of letters and sounds without vital connection to feeling. Poets, with their words, can be among the custodians of this beautiful earth. They can be custodians of endangered elements of culture, too; of humanistic and ethnic traditions that may be lost in the digital world of easy, fast information and hurried opinion.

In my poems, I work to celebrate the gifts of this earth and to bear witness to connectedness and the pulsing movement of nature through our lives.

OUR DAUGHTER WRITES FROM ACROSS THE WORLD

There in Papua New Guinea
nightfall comes early and is thick with black.
In giant trees outside her house,
flying foxes crash from branch to branch,
wings sounding Clap! Clap! Clap!
throughout the starry night.

Here's what hibiscus does—
it unfurls its beauty with light,
wraps it away in the dark,
each blossom a flame
flickering into night.

The new moon
is a kina shell, hanging
like a necklace in the sky.

Sina, small jet-black birds
have eyes circled in red.
There are hundreds in the giant busa tree—
it holds at least fifty large hanging nests
that look like pendulous breasts.

It's in the sky that sina take her breath away,
their feathers sun-tinged brilliant purple.
They soar and swoop to create in concert
clouds of movement shimmering the air.

And on clear, moonlit island nights,
sounds of sina sink into her dreams—
until dawn, how beautifully she flies.

NINE GREAT EGRETS

make a surprise appearance
at dusk on the pond by the path
we are accustomed to walking.
Oh, our good luck! In dissolving light,
they are bright white forms of length and curl.
They move on stilted legs.
Their long necks stretch and bend.
Their long beaks dip casually
into darkening water. Slight breeze.
Bird voices in the surrounding trees
are down to murmur, sweet little
chips of sound. In the distance,
the busy roar of freeway. Like
the egrets, we choose not to listen.
We will carry this scene home with us.
Nine Great Egrets will be lodged
within a sanctuary of our minds.
To be themselves, not metaphor.

IT QUICKENS THE HEART

to look at the photo—she's
standing on the edge of a saltwater marsh
close to the sea in South Carolina.
She is, her father writes, absorbed
in watch for dolphins and birds,
standing close to sunlit water,
small girl on alert.
She knows there is more in the world
than she can contain,
but she is quick to catch what she can
and she holds it deep within her.
Collector of nature's throwaway bits—
stones, pine cones, slivers of bark,
tattered twigs, arrays of leaves—
she is an artist,
rearranging the untidy world
into miniature, telling of whole.
In her backyard in New Mexico
she watches a turtle named Angel.
No wings for the stubby creature—
like this child, an angel of earth,
alive on her own ground.

CRICKET
For Frank Big Bear

He started to call his daughter Cricket when she was a baby. He noticed that when he changed her diapers, she rubbed her tiny feet together, brushing them like a cricket brushes its hind legs, one against another to make its sound. She was so quiet; her sounds, when she started to make them, were like little cricket chirps. So the nickname held, putting Cricket right in the midst of an abundant world of call and response, in an ever-transforming nature that held her Indian ancestors, a bear, an evening star, a dipping moon, rippling water, an amber sunset, the quiet stare of a fawn, the crunch of autumn and a small, still pool of sorrow. And the birds, the birds flying over, carrying messages from the sun. As she grew into a young woman, the things in that world interlocked like puzzle pieces, even in the city with its taxicabs and cement. They were held together by memory and dream, vines crisscrossing and climbing, summer nights gentle and warm, the music of chirping rising in crescendo, falling away in diminuendo.

HOW WE, TOO, BECAME HERMITS

We two

put on the mantle
of silence

became friends
with tall, spare

pines, became
nobodies

listening to
clamoring frogs

clattering birds
Woodpecker's tap

the wrap
of self peeling

off like
birch bark

stark
hermit-honed

exposed
to breeze, bright

light, crack
of dawn

rustle, rain, ruffle
muck of mud

we headed down
the path of solitude

Millie, the dog
running before us

her eyes pure,
blue, simple as sky.

MID-OCTOBER

Brooding clouds ready to weep.
A few days ago, sun enveloped trees
and wind bantered with leaves
in their downward float.

———

In this contrary season,
I am mindful of my father, how he said
a few months before his death
I am the last leaf on the tree
thinking of his six departed siblings,
gentle ghosts hovering
over the earthly landscape of family.

———

A blue heron and three white egrets have disappeared
from their customary spots in the Wood Lake marsh.
I half expect to see them there, apparitions walking
on water, as they always seemed to do,
companions to their own reflected images.

———

The days are darkening.
Cattails crackle dry and brown.
Muskrats are building winter lodges.
Amphibians hunker down, phantom spiderlings
shoot out their tiny threads of silk
to ride the wind. On the rope of the creaking bridge,
an amazing spider web, big as a platter,
tufts of cattail fluff caught in delicate threads.

———

After many years, we are home
~Ishkwa nibawa dasobiboon niiawind abiendad~
On White Earth Reservation the burning sage
plumes softly to heal, the thump of drum
is beat of heart. Those who were adopted out
come home. They are no longer ghosts.
They take their places in the sacred circle.
No beginning, no end.

———

Now is the season
of Falling Leaves Moon.
Binaakwe-glizis
Fallen leaves litter the path.
The Tai Chi teacher instructs:
Hold up the sky   Hold the moon

———

Down under, the other side of the world,
the door opens out into spring—
jacaranda trees, bare in winter,
now royally robed with purple.
Golden Wattle explodes in sunbursts
across the waiting land.

———

How is the world made whole?
We live always between
the mists of desolation
and the rising smoke of restoration.
Where is the liminal space where
the hidden comes into view
and the disappeared return,
no longer wearing masks?

CONTRIBUTORS

LISA BERG loves to read and write and due to good fortune and luck, gets to hear and see writing being done every day as the owner (just) of the Blue Moon Coffee Cafe in Minneapolis—turned 15 this October—that has been adopted by an active, writing crowd. Her book, *Coming Back to the World*, was published by Laurel in February of 2005.

ANNIE BREITENBUCHER is a freelance writer living in Minneapolis; her stories have previously appeared in the *Minneapolis Star Tribune*, where she worked for twenty-three years. Her first poetry collection, *Fortune*, was published by the Laurel Poetry Collective in 2006.

MARGOT FORTUNATO GALT's poetry is collected in the Laurel book *Between the Houses* (2004) and in numerous anthologies, recently *To Sing Along the Way: Minnesota Women Poets...* (2006) and *County Lines* (2008). She has also published five books of nonfiction, two on her work as a Minnesota/Dakota writer-in-the-schools: *The Story in History* (1992) and *Circuit Writer* (2006) from Teachers & Writers Collaborative. With Ojibway artist George Morrison she created his oral-history memoir, *Turning the Feather Around: My Life in Art* (Minnesota Historical Society Press, 1998). Grants and awards from The Loft, the Jerome Foundation, the Minnesota State Arts Board, among others. Margot currently teaches at Hamline University, the University of Minnesota, and Metropolitan State University. See her website at http://mgalt.com.

ANN IVERSON received her MALS and MFA from Hamline University. She is the author of *Come Now to the Window*, Laurel Poetry Collective, and *Definite Space*, Holy Cow! Press. Her writing has been featured on *The Writer's Almanac* with Garrison Keillor and has appeared in *The Oklahoma Review*, *Margie: American Journal of Poetry*, *Water~Stone*, among many more. A visual artist, Ann takes interest in the intuitive and cyclical exchanges made between language and image. Currently, she is the Dean of Learning/Chief Academic Officer at Dunwoody College of Technology in Minneapolis. She and her husband live in East Bethel, Minnesota, and she is working on her third collection of poems, entitled *Art Lesson*.

MARY JUNGE lives and writes in Eden Prairie, Minnesota. Her poems have appeared in a variety of literary journals. *Express Train*, a poetry chapbook, was published by Pudding House Publications in 2002. *Pilgrim Eye*, a collection of poems, was published by the Laurel Poetry Collective in 2004. Everyday experiences, and encounters in the natural world, provide material for Junge's poems. The slowing that is required to create poems enables a welcome deepening of spirit.

Ghost Lamp is JOYCE KENNEDY's first collection of poetry. After a long career in education, the writing of poetry has become an integral part of her life. She lives in Richfield, Minnesota, near the Wood Lake Nature Center, where she and her husband Wallace walk the paths nearly every day when they are not visiting far-flung family members in Indiana, New Mexico, or Australia. Joyce recently finished a book of poetry about the women in William Shakespeare's plays, *Will's Women*.

ILZE KĻAVIŅA MUELLER is the author of *Gate*, published by Laurel in May of 2003. A native of Latvia, she divides her time between translation and poetry. Her poems have appeared in *Looking for Home: Women Writing About Exile*, *CALYX*, *Water~Stone*, *100 Words*, *Hedgebrook Journal*, and *Deeper Than You Think*, and her translations include Christa Reinig's *Idleness Is the Root of All Love* and texts in *The Review of Contemporary Fiction* (Spring 1998) and *Leading Contemporary Poets* (Western Michigan University).

EILEEN O'TOOLE lives in St. Paul, city of trees and poetry. She is the author of *Excerpts from Girl* (Laurel Poetry Collective, 2006) and *For the Purpose of Learning How to Breathe* (Cedar Fence Press), a fine-press chapbook designed by Regula Russelle. To learn where you can find poetry on the sidewalks of St. Paul, visit publicartstpaul.org.

TOM RUUD is the author of *Unable for the World to Sleep*, published by Laurel in 2005. He has published poems in *Southern Poetry Review*, *100 Words*, *Prairie Fire*, *Flyway*, *Minnesota Monthly*, *Mankato Poetry Review*, *Water~Stone*, and elsewhere. Awards, all in poetry, include: Minnesota State Arts Board Fellowship, Loft Mentor Series, and Lake Superior Regional Writers Competition. He teaches at The Loft in Minneapolis and privately (Monday Poets, which meets in Saint Paul). He lives with his wife Sylvia (dba Ytterli Press; she is artist designer and production editor of all the Laurel books) and two dogs, Sparky and Pepper, in Saint Paul.

SU SMALLEN is the author of *Weight of Light* (Laurel Poetry Collective, 2004), which was nominated for the Pushcart Press Editor's Book Award. Her many honors include the Jane Kenyon Poetry Prize, judged by Elizabeth Alexander, and grants from the Southeastern Minnesota Arts Council. Her poems and essays have appeared in *Bellingham Review*, *Bloom*, *Journal of Graduate Liberal Studies*, *Midway Journal*, *The Normal School*, *Saint Paul Almanac*, *Smartish Pace*, *three candles*, *Water~Stone Review*, and several anthologies.

SUZANNE SWANSON, author of *House of Music*, works in St. Paul, Minnesota, as a psychologist specializing in pregnancy, postpartum, and mothering. Suzanne contributed to the collaborative chapbook *The Part of Us That Craved the World* and is sole author of another chapbook, *What Other Worlds: Postpartum Poems*. She has been published in many literary journals, most recently, *Water~Stone*. Since 2005, Suzanne has been the creator of the Word section of Celtic contemplative services at Pilgrim Lutheran Church in St. Paul.

NANCY WALDEN is delighted with both the work and the play of writing poetry. She is the author of the book *In the Tent Called Amazement*. Nancy is a letterpress printer and one of the broadside artists for the Laurel Poetry Collective. She has an MFA in creative writing from Hamline University.

NOLAN ZAVORAL wrote journalism for more than twenty years as a staff writer for the *Milwaukee Journal*, *USA Today* and the *Minneapolis Star Tribune*. He holds an M.S. in Journalism from Northwestern University, Evanston, Ill., and an MFA in Young Adult and Children's Writing from Hamline University, St. Paul, Minn. His nonfiction book, the critically acclaimed *A Season on the Mat (Dan Gable and the Pursuit of Perfection)*, from Simon & Schuster, has been reprinted, and follows an Iowa icon in his last season as the University of Iowa wrestling coach. A founding member of the Laurel Poetry Collective, Nolan has published one book of poetry from Laurel, *The Heretic Hotel*, and has had several poems published in Laurel anthologies and in other forums.